Blastoff! Readers are carefully developed by literacy experts to build reading stamina and move students toward fluency by combining standards-based content with developmentally appropriate text.

Level 1 provides the most support through repetition of high-frequency words, light text, predictable sentence patterns, and strong visual support.

Level 2 offers early readers a bit more challenge through varied sentences, increased text load, and text-supportive special features.

Level 3 advances early-fluent readers toward fluency through increased text load, less reliance on photos, advancing concepts, longer sentences, and more complex special features.

★ **Blastoff! Universe**

This edition first published in 2024 by Bellwether Media, Inc.

No part of this publication may be reproduced in whole or in part without written permission of the publisher. For information regarding permission, write to Bellwether Media, Inc., Attention: Permissions Department, 6012 Blue Circle Drive, Minnetonka, MN 55343.

Library of Congress Cataloging-in-Publication Data

Names: Anderson, Shannon, 1972- author.
Title: Costa Rica / by Shannon Anderson.
Description: Minneapolis, MN : Bellwether Media, Inc., 2024. | Series: Blastoff! Readers : Countries of the world | Includes bibliographical references and index. | Audience: Ages 5-8 | Audience: Grades 2-3 | Summary: "Relevant images match informative text in this introduction to Costa Rica. Intended for students in kindergarten through third grade"– Provided by publisher.
Identifiers: LCCN 2023046586 (print) | LCCN 2023046587 (ebook) | ISBN 9798886877922 (library binding) | ISBN 9798886878868 (ebook)
Subjects: LCSH: Costa Rica–Juvenile literature.
Classification: LCC F1543.2 .A54 2024 (print) | LCC F1543.2 (ebook) | DDC 972.86–dc23/eng/20231018
LC record available at https://lccn.loc.gov/2023046586
LC ebook record available at https://lccn.loc.gov/2023046587

Text copyright © 2024 by Bellwether Media, Inc. BLASTOFF! READERS and associated logos are trademarks and/or registered trademarks of Bellwether Media, Inc.

Editor: Rachael Barnes   Series Design: Gabriel Hilger   Book Designer: Kathleen Petelinsek
Printed in the United States of America, North Mankato, MN.

Table of Contents

All About Costa Rica	4
Land and Animals	6
Life in Costa Rica	12
Costa Rica Facts	20
Glossary	22
To Learn More	23
Index	24

All About Costa Rica

San José

Costa Rica is a small country in **Central America**.

It is known for its beautiful **rain forests**. Its capital is San José.

San José, Costa Rica

Land and Animals

Costa Rica has many mountains. Some are **volcanoes**! A large **plateau** lies between them.

Rain forests cover about half of the land. Beaches line the west and east coasts.

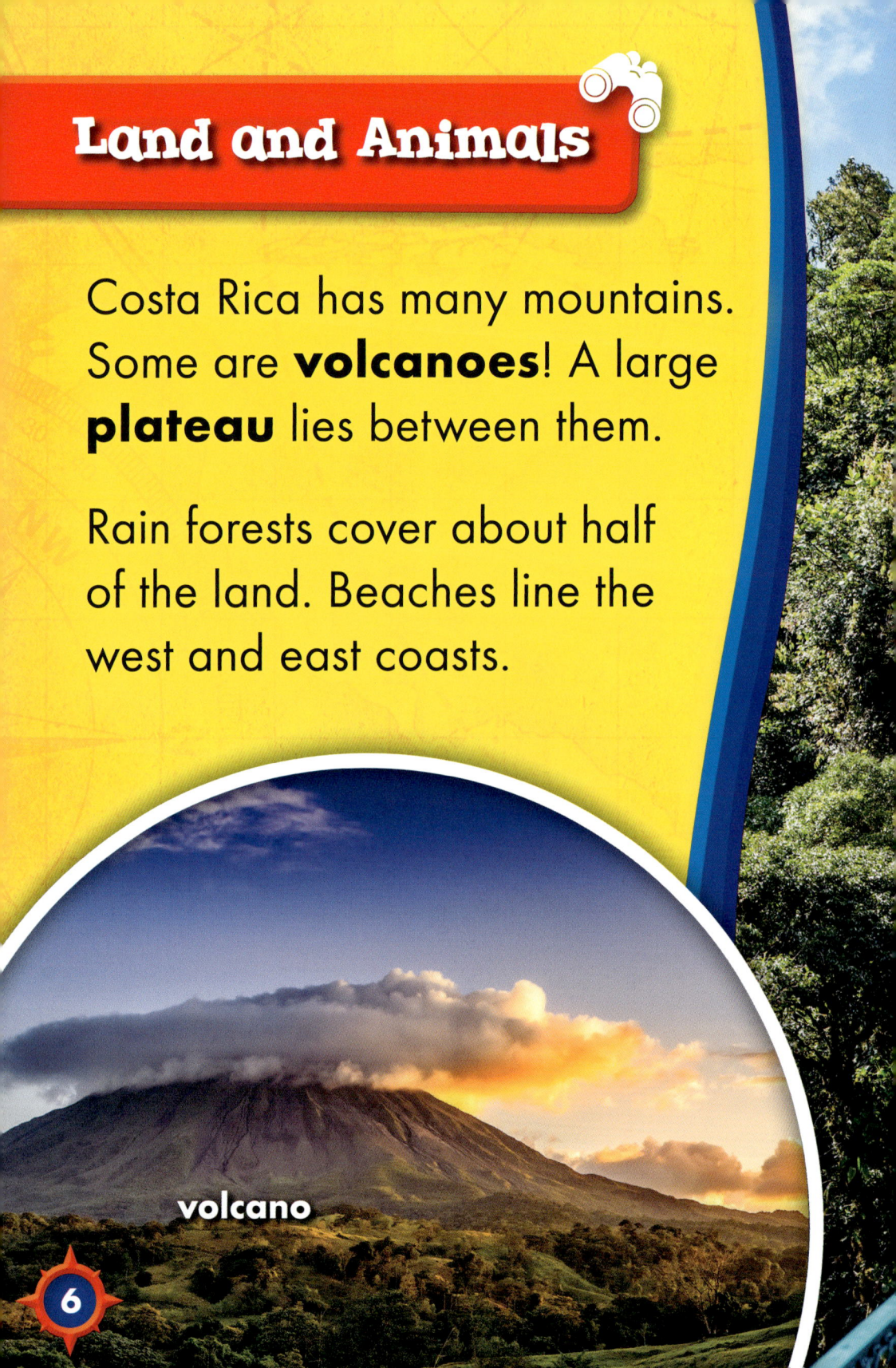

volcano

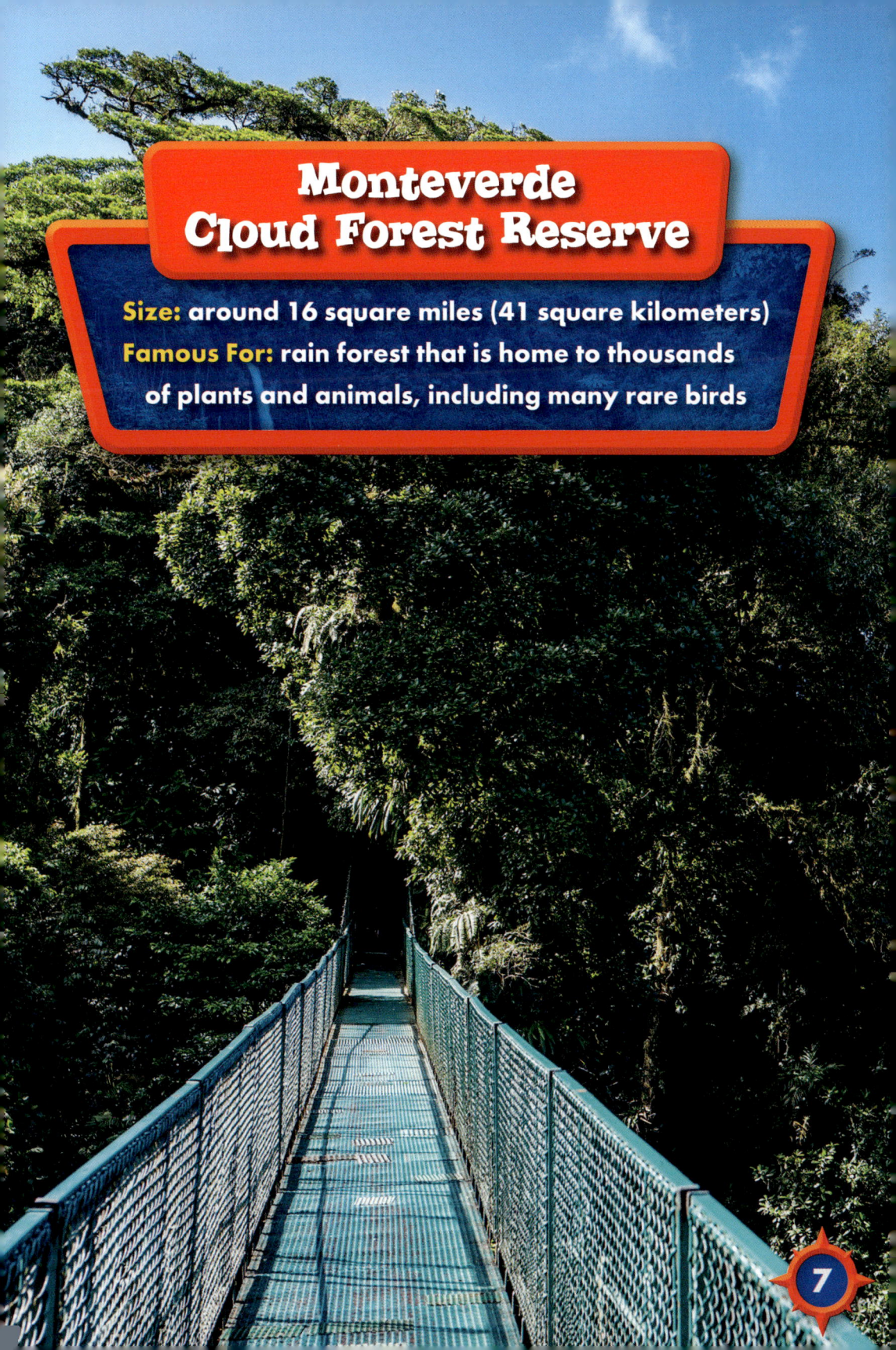

Monteverde Cloud Forest Reserve

Size: around 16 square miles (41 square kilometers)

Famous For: rain forest that is home to thousands of plants and animals, including many rare birds

The country is hottest near the coasts. The plateau is milder. It is cool in the mountains.

Most rain falls between May and November.

Many animals live in the rain forests. Howler monkeys and sloths hang in tall trees.

brown-throated sloth

Animals of Costa Rica

mantled howler monkey

brown-throated sloth

red-eyed tree frog

keel-billed toucan

Colorful frogs rest on tree trunks. Toucans call from high branches.

Life in Costa Rica

Costa Ricans speak Spanish with an **accent**. Boys are nicknamed *Ticos*. Girls are *Ticas*.

Most people live in cities. Many people are **Catholics**.

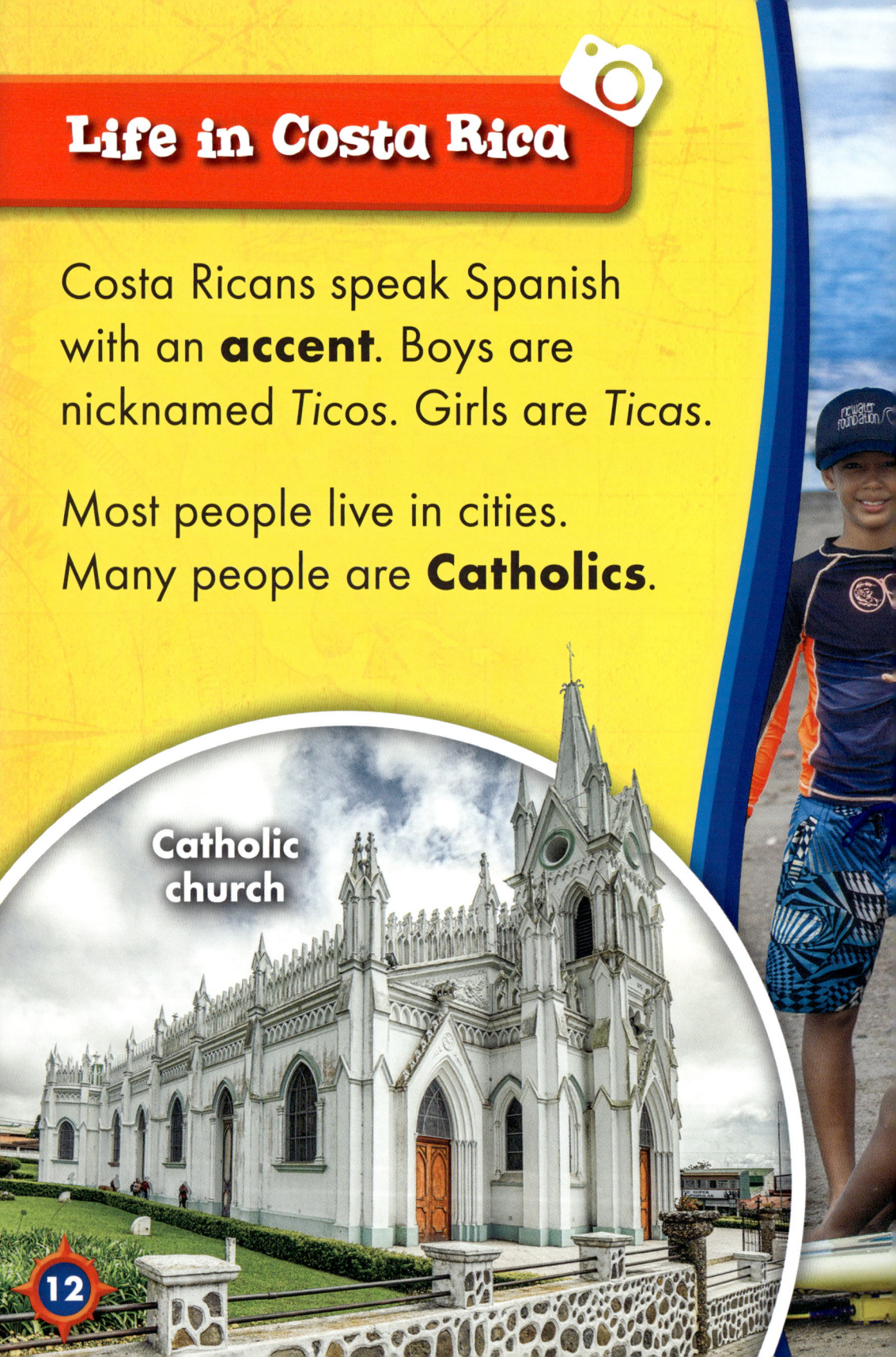

Catholic church

hiking

Costa Ricans like to spend time outside. Many people surf and hike.

Soccer and baseball are popular sports. Some people enjoy **Latin** dancing!

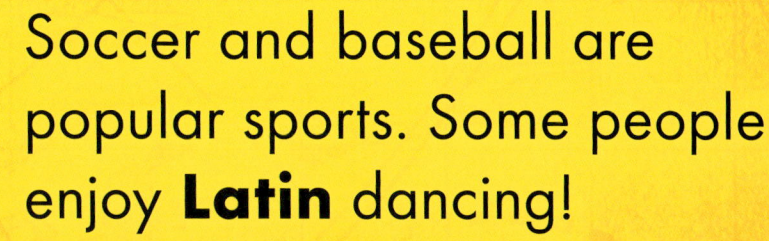

soccer

Latin dancing

Gallo pinto is a rice and black beans dish. Fried plantains are a tasty snack. *Rondón* is a seafood and vegetable stew.

Costa Rican Foods

gallo pinto

fried plantains

rondón

refrescos

Refrescos are drinks made with fruit and milk.

Independence Day

Independence Day is on September 15. People wave flags and enjoy parades.

Semana Santa is a Catholic holiday. Costa Ricans go to church. They spend time with family!

Costa Rica Facts

Size:
19,730 square miles
(51,100 square kilometers)

Population:
5,256,612 (2023)

National Holiday:
Independence Day (September 15)

Main Language:
Spanish

Capital City:
San José

Famous Face

Name: Harry Shum Jr.

Famous For: actor, dancer, and singer best known for his roles in *Shadowhunters* and *Glee*

Religions

- Roman Catholic 48%
- other Christian 22%
- none 27%
- other 3%

Top Landmarks

Irazú Volcano

Nicoya Peninsula

Tortuguero National Park

Glossary

accent—a way of talking shared by a group of people

Catholics—people belonging to or relating to the Christian church that is led by the pope

Central America—the narrow, southern part of North America; this region includes Belize, Costa Rica, El Salvador, Guatemala, Honduras, Nicaragua, and Panama.

Latin—relating to the countries or peoples of Latin America; Latin America includes Mexico, Central America, South America, and some Caribbean islands.

plateau—an area of raised, flat land

rain forests—thick, green forests that receive a lot of rain

volcanoes—holes in the earth; when a volcano erupts, hot ash, gas, and melted rock called lava shoots out.

To Learn More

AT THE LIBRARY

Anderson, Corey. *Costa Rica*. New York, N.Y.: Bearport Publishing, 2020.

Buller, Laura. *Sloths*. New York, N.Y.: DK Publishing, 2019.

Spanier, Kristine. *Costa Rica*. Minneapolis, Minn.: Jump!, 2021.

ON THE WEB

FACTSURFER

Factsurfer.com gives you a safe, fun way to find more information.

1. Go to www.factsurfer.com.
2. Enter "Costa Rica" into the search box and click 🔍.
3. Select your book cover to see a list of related content.

Index

animals, 10, 11
baseball, 15
beaches, 6
capital (see San José)
Catholics, 12, 19
Central America, 4
cities, 12
coasts, 6, 8
Costa Rica facts, 20–21
dancing, 15
food, 16, 17
hike, 14
Independence Day, 18
map, 5
Monteverde Cloud Forest Reserve, 7
mountains, 6, 8
people, 12, 14, 15, 18, 19
plateau, 6, 8

rain, 9
rain forests, 5, 6, 7, 10
San José, 4, 5
say hello, 13
Semana Santa, 19
soccer, 15
Spanish, 12, 13
surf, 14
Ticas, 12
Ticos, 12
volcanoes, 6

The images in this book are reproduced through the courtesy of: Mihai-Bogdan Lazar, front cover; Nick Fox, pp. 2-3; railway fx, p. 3 (flag); Gianfranco Vivi, pp. 4-5; Sebastian Machado, p. 6; Simon Dannhauer/Alamy, pp. 6-7; Olga Gabay, pp. 8-9; Simon Dannhauer, p. 9; jdross75, pp. 10-11; Milan Zygmunt, p. 11 (mantled howler monkey); Rob Jansen, p. 11 (brown-throated sloth); worldswildlifewonders, p. 11 (red-eyed tree frog); Ondrej Prosicky, p. 11 (keel-billed toucan); Jarib Gonzalez, p. 12; Jorge A. Russell, pp. 12-13, 17; Galyna Andrushko, pp. 14-15; Luis Alvarado Alvarado, p. 15 (soccer); Nature's Charm, p. 15 (Latin dancing); LaMantarraya, p. 16 (*gallo pinto*); Ildi Papp, p. 16 (fried plantains); Cesar Okada, p. 16 (*rondón*); Aleat88/Wiki Commons, p. 16 (*refrescos*); Cara Koch, pp. 18-19; titoOnz, p. 20 (flag); Joe Seer, p. 20 (Harry Shum Jr.); Michal Sarauer, p. 21 (Irazú Volcano); Jeffry Gonzalez, p. 21 (Nicoya Peninsula); CL-Medien, p. 21 (Tortuguero National Park); Dirk Ercken, p. 22.